From Remedial To Remarkable

Ralph L. Simpson, Ed.D.

EDUCATION PUBLISHING SERVICES

From Remedial To Remarkable
by Ralph L. Simpson, Ed.D.

Published by:
ItsMyCareer Education Publishing Services
Atlanta, Georgia 30339
www.ItsMyCareerActivityBooks.com

Copyright © 2018 Ralph L. Simpson, Ed.D.

All Rights Reserved. No part of this publication may be reproduced, stored in or introduced into a retrieval system, or transmitted, in any form, or by any means (recording, electronic, photocopying, or otherwise), without the prior written permission of both the copyright owner and publisher of this book.

ISBN 978-0-692-62463-0

FIRST EDITION: January 2018
10 9 8 7 6 5 4 3 2 1

PUBLISHER'S NOTE
The scanning, uploading, and distribution of this book via the Internet or via any other means without the permission of the publisher or author is illegal and punishable by law. Please purchase only authorized editions. Your support of the author's rights is appreciated.

From Remedial To Remarkable books are available at quantity discounts when utilized to promote products or services.

In Loving Memory

My maternal grandparents, Ms. Roxie Shannon and Mr. Arthur B. Shannon, for raising twelve children the right way.

My paternal grandfather Henry Simpson, for being a true patriarch.

My late father, Henry Simpson, Jr., for being a true inspiration and a fine example for hard work and determination.

Dedication

To my mother, Ms. Roxie Mae Simpson, my father, Henry Simpson Jr., my brother, Henry J. Simpson: thanks for supporting me in all my endeavors.

To my children, Chandler and Skyla: I promise to care for you with all my might and heart. You have changed my life forever and I love you.

Acknowledgments

To the Shannon/Simpson family: Thanks for all the love, support, and nurturing.

To my best friends, Tony Owens, Al Ringer, and Kevin Ware: You brothers keep me grounded and have consistently been my role models.

To Reverend Timothy McDonald and the entire First Iconium Baptist Church: Thanks for being my spiritual leader in providing undying support.

To Dawn Price: The title "From Remedial to Remarkable" was your idea; thanks.

To Quarnitra McClinton: As a long time advisor and avid reader, thanks for your suggestions and ideas.

To the brothers of Omega Psi Phi Fraternity, Incorporated, especially Kappa Kappa Chapter, for making me believe that anything is possible through Manhood, Scholarship, Perseverance, and Uplift.

To Dr. Percy Mack and Mike Hall: Thanks for being my mentor and guardian angel.

To Dr. Brenda Emerson: Thanks for recognizing my leadership potential and supporting me.

To my editors, Dr. Roberta Maxwell, Nalini Babb and Tomika Moody: Thanks for your wonderful critique of my work.

To my illustrators, Sheila Bussey and Christopher Walker: Thanks for your creativity.

To my Media Specialists, Cora Lima and Jean Bailey: Thanks for promoting me.

And finally, to God be the glory, who is worthy of my honor and praise every day: Thanks for blessing me with the ability to do what I do!

Introduction

I felt compelled to write this book because I would like to share my story with others about how I was able to go from taking remedial courses in high school and college to remarkably completing the highest educational degree. Let it be known that I do realize that what is most remarkable is how much God has blessed me with the desire, dedication, willingness, and determination to persevere regardless of the challenges I have faced. What I have done is something that can be done by anyone. I truly believe that I am just an ordinary person who has always attempted to do extraordinary things.

This is a book for those who do not like to read. This is the type of book for easy readers, a book that can be read within 24 hours. This is for the people who have never read a book in their lives. In addition, this book is written for those who were never recognize for academic abilities. As you continue to read, you will see that according to research, I should not have graduated from college. Based upon my SAT scores I should have never earned a Bachelor's,

Master's, Specialist's, or Doctorate degree. That is the reason why I feel that this book will serve as a blueprint for how to do it and will validate the fact that if I did it, anybody can.

In all honesty, I hated school and everything associated with it. I do understand how and why one can grow tired of studying, taking tests, and doing projects. Writing these words fosters a sickening feeling in my stomach when I think of all that you might have to go through. Although I took a while, I was able to realize something extremely important. When I discovered and understood that education was a means to my success, everything appeared to be pretty easy.

Contents

I Hate School   1

Algebra I   9

Failure 2 Prepare is Preparing 2 Fail   15

13th Grade   21

The Frat   29

Tuition   37

The Lock Up   43

Standing 4 Something   51

Lean On Me   57

Get In The Way   65

Braggin' Rights   75

Conclusion   81

"We must become the change we want to see in the world."

Mahatma Gandhi

Chapter One

I Hate School

Just because you go to school every day is not a guarantee you are going to make good grades. Although I had a perfect attendance in grades K-12, I was never ever recognized from my academic ability. I did not take full advantage of spending that much time in a learning environment. Not only did I hate school, I did not like the smart kids. I am talking about the students that had all the correct answers to all the questions. Remember this though, "If you hate them in school, you will hate on them later on in life." Like them or not, they will be the ones riding how you want to ride. They will also be living how you want to live. Picture this, "Cars and Clothes,

Twenty Fours." It does not really matter where you are now, but what matters more is where you will be in 10 or 15 years from now.

In my first year of high school (as an 8th grader), I did not take books home for an entire school year. In my mind, it was cool not to have any books in your hands after school. In my mind, it was easier to talk to the girls without having books in your hand.

Although I could read, I did not read for enjoyment. I can recall my 4th grade teacher, Ms. Banks, calling on students to read aloud. If you could not read, your classmates "joned" you forever. As a matter of fact, I did not read a book from cover to cover from grades 8-12. I never did a book report or research paper in high school. When I had homework, I would get to school early enough to copy it from a friend. That was the easiest way to get by. I never studied or prepared. I hated everything about what school represented. What was best about being in high school was the GIRLS. I completely lost my mind when I saw all the pretty girls that attended

Southwest High School (Atlanta). This school has a very rich tradition and was often recognized for its academic and athletic excellence. However, that did not mean much to me at all. The band, football team, and basketball team were the bomb. Oh, I failed to mention the cheerleaders.

During the summer months when school ended, my brother and I were not allowed to stay in the house unsupervised. We had to do something! We began going to summer school when I was in the 4th grade. From that time until I became a senior, I attended summer school all but one summer. During that time, you could go to summer school to get ahead.

At the completion of my 10th grade year, I had enough credits to graduate from high school. However, someone told me that if I had plans on going to college, I should continue taking Math and Science. I had no plans on going to college at that time; therefore, I put very little effort into classes that I took. For the record, I enjoyed my yearbook, newspaper,

JROTC, Spanish, and P.E. classes. I would always earn a good grade. However, I never came close to making the Principal's List of Honor Roll. I chose to do just enough work to get by. A grade of "C", in my opinion, meant I was "Cool". Instead of being the most talked about, I was the most talkative. This earned me a grade of "F" in conduct for all my classes except Physical Education. Now, that was a class that made sense. My first report card was so bad that I changed the "D" and "F's" to "B's". Back then, report cards were issued on stencil paper, which made it easier to change a grade. I never showed my mom a report card after the 8th grade. She must have assumed that I was passing because I was promoted to the next grade. One thing for sure, I knew that some work had to be done.

There were few things that did motivate me to do a little work. As a 12th grader, you could serve as a Hall Monitor. That meant that you stood in the hallway for an entire class period checking for student passes. I could not wait to get that opportunity.

In addition, at my high school, it was a tradition for the junior and senior classes to display their talents by wearing their class colors and entering the gymnasium full of students dancing to the hottest songs. It was basically an hour long party for the junior and senior classes. I look forward to leading my classmates out of that door getting my dance on.

Whatever motivates you to go to school and do some work, go for it.

"I hated every minute of training, but I said, 'don't quit'. Suffer now and live the rest of your life as a champion."

Muhammad Ali

Chapter Two

Algebra I

For those of you who do not know, Math is a building process. It becomes more difficult if you do not grasp the necessary concepts at each level. For example, if Algebra I was difficult for you, Geometry will likely give you fits. As an 8th grader taking Algebra I, I began to struggle. Because I did not want to feel embarrassed by asking questions, I fell further and further behind. There was no way I was going to look like an idiot amongst my peers especially when there was a girl in the class whom I liked. Because of that, I never asked questions. Homework was very difficult for me. If I could not solve the first Math equation, I became frustrated and quit. I was totally confused by the time I returned for class the next day.

I ended up with a grade of "D" in Algebra I. I earned the grade because I turned in all of my homework that I copied from a friend. Well, next year was Geometry and as you might imagine, I bombed. I continued to miss those critical steps and concepts along the way. This was the result of my weak skills from Algebra I. I continued the practice of copying homework and earned a "D" in Geometry. To make a long story short, I earned a "D" in every Math class and grades 8-12. All of this resulted in one of the most embarrassing and disappointing times in my life.

My first college Math course in which I would earn credit resulted in a grade of D. Because of my low grade point average, I decided to wait and take the next required Math class the last semester of my senior year. That was a big mistake. I do not take a Math class for two years. As I approached my last semester, I enrolled in this class and received a grade of 56 on my first two exams. Because I desperately needed to pass the class in order to graduate, I attended the Math Lab and had a tutor for additional assistance. I still struggled tremendously! I never passed one test during the entire class. Anticipating graduation, I ordered my cap and gown as well as sent out invitations to family members. Had I earned at least a "D", I would have graduated. The professor told me that I needed to make the grade of 83 or better to get a "D" out of the class. The final exam would cover twelve chapters. Reality set in when I realized that I had not earned an 83 to test that covered just one chapter. I passed the final exam with a grade of 76 and failed the class. My mother knew that I was struggling in this class, but remained prayerful that I would pull it out. I would never forget walking into the house that rainy day and being asked what time was graduation. I replied, "There will be a graduation, but I will not be a part of it."

    Because of my friends and Fraternity brothers graduating, I attended the ceremony. When I walk into the gymnasium, I was handed a program. I was shocked to find my name listed as a candidate for graduation. As I prepared to take my seat, I encountered many of my peers that asked why was I not graduating as anticipated. I shared with them that I failed my Math class. Now, let's go back! Remember that eighth grade algebra I class? Again, I stress to you that Math as a building process. If you don't get it now, it will come back to haunt you later. I enrolled to take this same class the following semester and earned a "B" to complete my graduation requirements.

"You have got to start with a plan. I was in school, I took architectural drafting and that taught me that everything starts with a plan. The biggest buildings in the world start with a plan. You've got to have determination, the talent, and you have to recognize opportunities to seize the moment."

Ice Cube

Chapter Three

Failure 2 Prepare is Preparing 2 Fail

"Without a TEST, there is no TESTIMONY!" Because I had not imagined or believed that I would be faced with making a decision like going to college, I was not serious about taking the SAT. Just in case you did not know, this is the test that helps determine a couple of things. One, if you will be admitted to college, and two, how much it will cost you. In my mind, I knew that I would have to face this, but in reality, I made every attempt to avoid it. It is supposed to determine whether you can really handle the college level work. I did not place a whole lot of emphasis on the SAT because I was not planning on going to college anyway.

The idea is to get as close to a perfect score to increase your chances of attending college on an academic scholarship as well as having a variety of colleges to choose from. Today a perfect score on the SAT is 2400. When I was graduating from high school, it was 1600. College Board has added an essay course to the SAT. Before I could even consider college, I first had to take the SAT. Because I had no intentions on going to college, I did nothing to prepare for this test. I missed the registration deadline and had to pay a late fee. I eventually took it on a Saturday morning after attending a party the night before.

My score on the SAT was far beyond embarrassment. To begin, they give 200 points for your name. With the 200 free points, I earned 280 additional points for a total of 480. Even in 1981, a score of 480 on the SAT was ridiculous. Well, I applied for college regardless of my score, and much to my surprise, I was accepted to attend West Georgia College three weeks before school started.

Wherever you are in your desire to get an education, you are probably tired of taking tests. I have some bad news to share with you, tests have been around for a long time and will continue for a long time to come, so get over it and get it done. "Failure to prepare is like preparing to fail." At every instance, you should take advantage of an opportunity to be a successful test taker. In my mind, I believed that I did not test well. I spent too much time convincing myself that I was not a good test taker instead of preparing for the test. I never studied or prepared for the SAT. I do not enroll in a SAT prep program. Poor scores are a result of poor preparation.

As a senior, I felt like this would be the year for me to truly do nothing. My first semester schedule consisted of the following:

1st Period - Office Aid
2nd Period – Spanish II
3rd Period - JROTC
4th Period - Yearbook
5th Period - PE

6th Period – Office Aid

Was I ready for college or what? As a result, I graduated from high school without knowing how to study or take notes from a teacher lecture. Deep down, I was afraid. I looked forward to attending college for all the social aspects. I have heard that West Georgia College was a party school, which sounded like a perfect place for me to be. I was faced with making a decision knowing that I was not prepared to do work in the college level.

Prior to enrolling at West Georgia College and because of my low scores on the SAT, I had to take a Placement Exam that tests the basic skills in Math, Reading, and English. As a result of my scores, it was mandatory that I had to take all three remedial courses. I was excited and was looking forward to the college experience. In my mind, it was time for me to party. Never in my wildest dreams would I have imagined that I will be in the 13th grade.

"If you live long enough, you'll make mistakes. But if you learn from them, you'll be a better person. It's how you handle adversity, not how it affects you."

Bill Clinton

Chapter Four

13th Grade

I spent an entire year in Developmental Studies or remedial courses. These classes do not earn credit toward graduation. That is likely to happen when you are not prepared for college. To make matters worse, the tuition for these classes is the same as a regular class that counts for graduation. The only way to exit the class is to first earn a Satisfactory (S) so that you can take the exam for that particular subject area. The passing score at the time was a 67.

Because I was accepted to WGC three weeks before school began, I was not able to register for any of these remedial courses. Believe it or not, they were completely full with my fellow 13th graders.

Therefore, I had to register for regular credit classes during my first semester.

My very first college course was a Political Science course that was taught by the president of West Georgia College, the late Dr. Maurice Townsend. I will never forget the level of fear and intimidation in addition to bad luck for being in a class taught by the president. My other two classes were Sociology and Speech Communications. At the end of the semester, my report card showed that I had earned two "C's" and a D. My grade point average was 1.67, and I was on "Academic Probation" after my first semester in college.

The next semester would serve as a wakeup call. If my grade point average did not rise above 2.00, I would have flunked out of college. By that time, I was a full-time 13th grader taking 099 Math, English, and Reading. I must point out that regular courses for credit started at 100. Notice to 099 distinctions. It was quite embarrassing to walk around campus with a big bold 099 stamped on your books with everyone knowing exactly what that meant. Needless to say, I was proud to be in 099 because deep down inside I needed to be there.

I can recall the first assignment in my English class when the professor asked all of the students to write about eight to ten sentences telling a little bit about ourselves. This was my opportunity to display my creative writing skills, so I used as many punctuation marks as I could. My paragraph included roughly ten sentences, and I handed it to the professor with pride knowing that it was good. When the professor returned it, there was more red ink on my paper than the blue ink that I had written in. That same professor pulled me aside after class and shared some startling information. He said, "Mr. Simpson, I am sorry to inform you sir that you cannot write. I responded by saying, "Sir, I know."

This was my first time hearing of the four major errors: writing fragments, run-on sentences, comma splices, and subject-verb agreements. At the end of the semester, I was allowed to take the Reading and

English exam. I failed to make a 67 on both sections, therefore, I had to register and take these classes the next semester. I did not take the Math exam because in order to take that exam, you had to complete the manual. I was stuck on the "Word Problems" chapter for four weeks.

At the end of the third semester, I took the skills exam for all three subjects. I finally passed the Math and English sections. I went into my second year of college still trying to get out of the remedial Reading class. During the first semester of the year, I passed the class.

While I thought this was all over, I was faced with another challenge a few years later. When you become a Junior, all students must take and pass the Georgia Regents Exam. This exam covers two areas, Reading Comprehension and Writing. If a student fails either section, it is mandatory that he or she register for the remedial course for the area failed. The first time I took the Regents Exam as a junior, I failed both sections, and I registered for what I now call Advanced Remedial Courses. At the end of this semester, the student is given an opportunity to take the test again. The following is a list of the number of times I took remedial or advanced remedial courses without any credit toward graduation along with the total cost of money that was wasted:

Remedial (as a result of poor scores on the Placement Exam and SAT).

   Math - 2 semesters

   English - 2 semesters

   Reading - 4 semesters

Advanced Remedial (result of failing the Georgia Regents Exam)

   Reading Comprehension – 1 semester

   Writing - 2 semesters

With each class costing about $200.00, I spent a total of $2,000.00 on classes that did not count. Again, "Failure to prepare is like preparing to fail". This was a result of "Senioritis" as well. Remember the schedule that I had as a 12th grader? While I was spending time learning the latest dance steps and spending an entire class period in the hallway, I should have been taking classes that would have better prepared me for college. I always wondered what students did to get skipped. One thing I do know is that you need to skip the 13th grade.

"A setback is a setup for a comeback."

Willie Jolley

Chapter Five

The Frat

Early into my freshman year as I enjoyed all that college had to offer, I made it my business to be at every party, step-show, or gathering of people. My only reason for going to college in the first place was to hang out with some of my old high school buddies. For the first three weeks of school, I attended a party every night. However, it was at a party for incoming students where I observed a group of men that would change my life forever.

I was on the dance floor when a group of guys all wearing purple and gold colors with gold boots and dog collars around their necks came on the dance floor. To add to it, they were barking like dogs and yelling chants that were on beat with the music. It was the wildest thing I had seen, yet intriguing. I went to my seat after the girl that I was dancing with left me and started dancing with one of them. I guess she was just as intrigued with these guys as I was.

As I sat there, I could tell by her response that whoever they were, she was impressed with them. The days following, I began to do a little homework to find out who and what these guys are all about. I discovered that the "Que Dogs" is an informal name that they used, but the formal name of the organization is Omega Psi Phi Fraternity, Incorporated.

Before this point, I saw no other reason for college except for the partying. Finally, I had discovered something of which I could become a part. However, I knew that it could not be that easy. After seeing the announcement for those interested in becoming members, I decided to make my interest known.

While sitting in a room full of prospective members, I listened to the history of this organization and the principles upon which they were founded.

They began to talk about Manhood, Scholarship, Perseverance, and Uplift as prerequisites. I did not have a problem with three of the principles, but the one about Scholarship I feared would cause me some problems. Well, as you can imagine, it did.

One of the criteria for interested members was that you must hold at least a 2.5 grade point average or better. This was my first semester in school and I was having a difficult time. With a 1.67 GPA, I had to watch other interested members become fully initiated into Omega Psi Phi Fraternity. From that point, I made it my business to buckle down and hit the books. College became about being a Que Dog and nothing else. That did not include graduating from college.

Surprisingly enough, I was motivated to seriously bring up my grade point average. I had found something in my mind that was worth doing some work for. Becoming a member of this Fraternity was my goal. Nothing was going to get in the way of this dream coming true. I started studying at the library and even on weekends. At the same time, I made sure that I supported all of the Omega Psi Phi Fraternity events.

It took one full year to obtain the required 2.5 grade point average to be a candidate for initiation. In the winter of 1983, I started on the journey to become a man of Omega. After eight long weeks, I was initiated and felt that I accomplished all that life offered. In my mind, there was nothing left for me to do. I felt that I now had a license to be as wild and crazy as possible. Graduating from college was the furthest thing from my mind. It was not until an older Fraternity brother who became my mentor invited me to his home. I was quite impressed by his standard of living. He drove a pretty nice car, too. I asked him how he had obtained these things. David Dennis, or D.D., as he was affectionately known, shared with me that graduating from college and working within his field had assisted him in obtaining a nice home and pretty nice car.

Until that moment, I had never realized how

important education was to my future. Remember, I went to college just to hang out with a group of friends. I lacked the motivation to study and do all the things necessary to graduate from college. This was the very first time in my life when I was faced with having to work for something. My motivation was to become a member of this Fraternity. That same motivation led me to study and make good grades. After being initiated, I truly felt that I could accomplish anything I set my mind to. Graduation began to seem like more of a reality.

Many of my Fraternity brothers who had graduated came to visit on a frequent basis. I had a chance to hear from these brothers about how they were living. I was definitely impressed with their success stories. As graduation became even more possible, I cannot help but think of how I had gotten this far.

Had it not been for the high standards to become a part of Omega Psi Phi Fraternity, I wonder if I truly would have begun to take school more seriously. Although I was mostly attracted to it because of the social aspects, I learned over a period of time that ALL ACHIEVERS ARE OMEGA, AND ALL OMEGAS ARE ACHIEVERS.

"You may not get all that you work for, but you will work for everything that you get."

Booker T. Washington

Chapter Six

Tuition

A year after my first year of college, I decided to capitalize off of being a social butterfly. I knew a lot of people and there were probably more people that knew me. I decided to have a party in my backyard during the summer. It was advertised by word of mouth. I rented a parachute to cover the entire backyard just in case it rained. In addition, I went to all of my neighbors within a block to let them know that I was having a party and that there might be a lot of people and traffic.

To my surprise, there were over one thousand people that showed up for a party in the backyard. The admission was $1.00. After paying the DJ, I profited about $700.00. While this started out as just something to do, I decided to take it to another level and pay my tuition at the same time.

As the holiday was approaching and the end of the semester, I decided to rent out some space near downtown Atlanta to host a Christmas party. Again, the advertisement was strictly by word of mouth. The only difference is that the admission was $5.00. After paying for security, DJ, and the money that my dad loaned me to rent the place, I had made enough money to go back and pay my winter semester tuition. At the end of the winter semester, I did the exact same thing at the same place and made enough money to pay for my spring tuition. At the end of the spring semester, I repeated again to pay for my summer tuition. To make a long story short, I held a party at the end of every semester to pay my tuition for the next three years while I was in college.

Being a popular person had some privileges. There is no way I would have been able to do this without flyers or radio advertisements and make enough money to pay for college. Oh, I must add that I was able to pay my rent at the same time.

I have heard of people having rent parties, but not many had tuition parties. I was blessed with being able to bring a lot of people together even if it was for the purpose of partying. It has been said that you have to use what you got to get what you want. Without knowing, I was able to do something that I did not know I could do.

"There is in this world no such force as the force of a man determined to rise. The human soul cannot be permanently chained."

W.E.B. Dubois

Chapter Seven

The Lock Up

In March of 1986, I graduated from West Georgia College with a 2.14 grade point average. By the grace of God, I walked out of there with a degree in Criminal Justice and high hopes of becoming a Secret Service, Federal Bureau of Investigation, or Drug Enforcement Agent. In order to be considered, you had to pass the Treasury Enforcement Exam. For some reason I could not seem to get away from those tests. However, this one included a large number of mathematical equations, word problems to be specific. As a result of those already poor math skills, I did not pass the test.

During the summer of 1986, I was asked by a

friend to take him to a job interview. He was interviewing for a Corrections Officer position at Metro Correctional Institution, a maximum-security prison. As I sat in the lobby waiting for him to finish his interview, I started a conversation with the officer working the reception desk. She asked me what I was doing. I shared with her that I had just graduated from college with a degree in Criminal Justice. She encouraged me to apply for Correctional Officer I position at the prison. As I sat there waiting and wasting time, it did not sound like a bad idea. I applied and was called for an interview a few weeks later. In November of 1986, after completing a month in the training academy, I became Officer Simpson.

After hearing and seeing all of the horror stories about prison life, this was the last place I thought I would have ended up working. I was assigned to a cellblock for newly arrived inmates. I was excited and enthusiastic about my new experience. Immediately, I established a rapport with the inmates that was based on mutual respect. Listening to some of their stories, I was truly blessed that I had made some good decisions. The inmates would always tell me that this was not the place for a kid such as myself with a college degree. Nevertheless, I learned a lot about what not to do and at the same time felt sorry for those whose families did not come to visit or write them.

After being there for eighteen months, I transferred to a halfway house. Over the next six months or so, I became interested in becoming a Probation Officer. I was interviewed for this position thirteen times and was unsuccessful. Shortly thereafter, I left the state prison system and became employed with the City of Atlanta as a Corrections Officer.

During the late 80's and 90's, the crack cocaine epidemic was in full swing. As I worked at the back door (Intake), I witnessed vans loaded to capacity with African American males being brought to jail 15-20 at a time. A lot of times, they were packed in like sardines. This was the routine for a Friday night. The floors that housed the inmates were disturbing.

Because of the over crowdedness in the jail, inmates were given the mattress and asked to sleep on the floor. In order to account for the inmates, we (officers) had to step over bodies to conduct roll call. The smell of the cell blocks was strong enough to make a person sick. There was a cloud of cigarette smoke thick enough to cut with a knife. This experience did not hit home until a close friend asked me a very interesting question. "Did you have a good day at work today?" he asked. I pause and then replied, "How and when is it a good day at work when over ninety percent of the inmates just look just like you?"

I began to notice the existing and overwhelming majority of African American males being arrested on a daily basis. Around the same time and as I began to look for answers to the problem, I stumbled across a book entitled, Countering the Conspiracy to Destroy Black Boys. The famous author, Dr. Jawanzaa Kunjufu, talked about the "Fourth Grade Failure Syndrome" that affects African American adolescent males and most importantly, the lack of African

American male teachers in the educational system throughout the country. After hearing Dr. Kunjufu speak at the Green Forrest Baptist Church in 1990, I decided to become a part of the solution instead of the problem. I went back to the WGC to seek a certification to teach middle grades 4-8.

After leaving the field of corrections, I would grow to appreciate it even more. Just think, if I had been promoted, I would have never had the opportunity to have an impact in the lives of children. Because they come in so many different shapes, sizes, and colors, I never judged a book by its cover. I treated every inmate ranging from those serving a one-year sentence or life in prison with common decency and respect. I was nicknamed "College Boy" by the inmates. They would always tell me that the Lock Up is no place for person like me with a college education. Many of the inmates share their stories. However, most of their comments were wishful thinking. Over and over again, the inmates wished for a chance at an instant replay about the decisions they made to land them behind bars.

My experiences while working in the Lock Up taught me to treat all individuals with kindness and respect. I felt the sharing these experiences with our youth might prevent a number of males from going down that road. I want to become the role model that they would see every day. In addition, this experience increased my desire and dedication to prevent young African American males from entering the prison system.

"Let us not become weary in doing good, for at the proper time, we will reap a harvest if we do not give up."

Galatians 6:9

Chapter Eight

Standing 4 Something

In the fall of 1990, I had worked as a Corrections Officer for nearly four years. I was hoping to be promoted by now, but for some reason it was not meant for me to be a Sergeant. Nevertheless, I was beginning to find my niche in life. I had to ask myself these questions "Ralph Simpson, why are you here? What is your purpose in life? What do you want to be known for?" Reading for knowledge and looking for answers to why there were so many African American males in the prison system, I decided to test something from a book written by Dr. Jawaanza Kunjufu as mentioned in the previous chapter.

I applied as a substitute teacher for the Atlanta

Public School System and was used mostly at my old high school that had been transformed into a middle school, Southwest Middle School initially. Later it was named after the late Jean Childs Young, wife of the Honorable Andrew Young. It was there that I posed a question to all males in the class. I wanted to see if there were any adults in a school setting that our boys actually looked up to. So, I asked if there was a man in this building that you see on a daily basis that you want to be like. I expected to hear the boys say that, "I want to be just like Mr. So and So," After polling every male student, each one of them stated that they did not aspire to be like any man in the entire school. Without a shadow of a doubt, I was going to become a teacher.

I was determined that education will be something that I would stand for. After obtaining a certification to teach middle school grades, I began teaching 5th graders at then Mainstreet Elementary School in the fall of 1991. Dr. Eldridge Miller was the principal at that time. He was my mentor, and I was grateful for the opportunity that he provided. Several years later, Dr. Miller became ill and passed away. The school was renamed in his honor, and I was eventually transferred to a middle school to teach 8th graders. At Mainstreet, I was the only African American male teacher on staff. The only other male staff member was Mr. Brandon Butler, with whom I quickly bonded. I will never forget the time we called in sick to go to a Braves baseball game. Dr. Miller was a very intelligent man. The next day at work, he asked us if we enjoyed the baseball game.

Most of all, I truly appreciated the molding and nurturing that I was provided by the female staff at Mainstreet. These women taught me how to teach. My first few years were difficult because I did not have a teaching background. I went from working in the prison to teaching my first class with twenty boys and nine girls without any formal teaching training. Finally, I was where I wanted to be. I immediately sponsored a male support group. Mr. Danny Buggs was founder of The Winning Circle. This organization focused on teaching boys to become men and was chartered at Mainstreet with approximately eighty boys. I felt that I was finally making a difference in the lives of children, particularly males. Because of low enrollment in October of 1994, I was transferred to Miller Grove Middle School.

"Reality is wrong. Dreams are for real."

Tupac Shakur

Chapter Nine

Lean On Me

By no stretch of the imagination, Lean On Me is one of my all-time favorite movies. Before I decided to become an educator, I felt the passion that Joe Clark, principal, had for the children of Eastside High School. My leadership style and the way I would run a school would be similar to the way Mr. Clark ran his. After teaching elementary and middle school for four years, I decided that it was time for me to pursue my Joe Clark vision. One of my mentors, Dr. Brenda Emerson, once told me that I needed to pursue administration. This was after she disciplined me for inappropriately dealing with a student. I can recall her telling me that if I wanted to become an administrator, then I should never allow a student to make me go left when I should go right. The most profound statement she made was that I needed to start "walking" like an administrator.

Although I did not understand that comment, I took it upon myself to look at how the administrators were walking. Interestingly enough, they did not walk any different from me. However, I think what she meant was I had better start conducting myself like a person who is ready to assume some leadership responsibilities.

Unfortunately, I would be faced with the challenge of taking another test to become accepted into a graduate program. Going back to college to obtain a master's degree required me taking the Graduate Record Exam or Miller Analogy Test. I registered to take the GRE and failed to meet the required score for admittance into graduate school at West Georgia College. Thinking that my chances would be better by taking the computer version, I registered for the online version and failed to meet the criteria once again. Now it was time for me to switch tests. I registered for the MAT and was unlucky with that one as well. With the scores that I had recorded, I applied for admittance into the graduate program anyway. My application was rejected because I had failed to meet the qualifying score on both tests. Refusing to quit, I enrolled in a MAT prep course at Emory University thinking that would help me get over the hump. Well, guess what, I failed once again to meet the required scores. In all, I took the GRE three times and the MAT two times and never qualified. I applied to West Georgia College once again and was rejected because of my scores on both tests. Once again, refusing to accept no for an answer, I appealed the decision to the Dean of Graduate Education, Dr. Jack Jenkins. How amazing was it that he remembered me from ten years ago when he was a Psychology professor and I was an out of control student. I can recall having a conversation with this man. After reviewing my undergraduate transcript, he stated that he had no evidence to prove I could handle the master's level coursework. I agreed with him but added that, "Ten years ago I was not the person I am today." I now understood that education is a means to my success.

Once again, all of my social activity came back to haunt me. I did my share of partying all those years if you recall. Well, after careful consideration and pleading, I was granted permission to enroll in the master's program on a probationary status. After eighteen months, I graduated from this program with a master's degree in Administration/Supervision.

While serving as a teacher at Miller Grove Middle School, an assistant principal was promoted to the position of principal in another school district. This took place a week before Spring Break. I knew how important it was to have a replacement.

I was given an opportunity to serve as an acting assistant principal for the remainder of the semester. I guess you could say that I was in the right place at the right time. In the fall of 1996, I was officially promoted to assistant principal at Miller Grove Middle

School where I served for the next two years. With my Joe Clark vision in sight, I made the jump to high school and became an assistant principal there. For two more years, I served in that capacity and in the fall of 2000, I became the first African American principal in the history of Stone Mountain High School.

For four years, I lived my dream providing leadership for students and teachers while working with parents and the community. With a background in the prison system, I truly believed that the climate must be controlled while creating an environment that is conducive for teaching and learning. In the spring of 2004, I was reassigned as principal to open the largest school in the history of the DeKalb County School System, Miller Grove High School.

"The educated of the 21st century will be he or she who can learn, unlearn, and relearn."

Alvin Toffler

Chapter Ten

Get In The Way

I once heard the legendary civil rights leader Joseph Lowery make a comment that we should get in the way of an education. At that time, I do not fully understand what he meant. He went on to add how important it is to obtain as much education as possible. I understand that to mean if you get in the way of an education, someone has to give you something to show for it. From K-12, I went to school every day (got in the way). For that, I received a high school diploma. For about five more years at West Georgia College, I got in the way. For that, I received a college degree. After all, I promised myself that I would never sit in another classroom as long as I live. At that point, I had gotten more education than I would have ever imagined. It is true when people say it is amazing how things happen. Somewhere along the way the light came on.

As I continue to grow and mature, I became more serious about my purpose in life. I had already returned to West Georgia on two separate occasions. I first returned to gain a certificate to teach middle grades and again to obtain a master's degree. A few years later, a few of my peers were enrolling in a doctoral program at the University of Sarasota. I was fed up with the idea of going back to school. I had already exceeded my educational expectations. The thought of sitting in a classroom with boring professors made me sick. I had promised myself that I would not write another paper, take another test, or do another project.

The University is Sarasota's criteria for admittance required the completion of the master's program along with an essay to state your interest. I was accepted, and for four more years, I got in the way. This was no easy task. It required traveling back and forth to Sarasota, Florida. Every break – Thanksgiving, Christmas, spring, and summer, I was taking classes. All classes started on Monday and ended on Friday from 9:00 AM to 5:00 PM. My biggest problem was sitting and listening to a professor for eight hours. As much as I hated school, this almost drove me to quit.

Being a first year principal and juggling school was kicking my butt. In November of the same year, my first child, Chandler, was born. Not only was I learning how to be a principal, I was also learning how to be a parent. I was faced with making a major decision. Something had to go! I decided that I would put school on hold for a while. Although I had no plans on quitting for good, I just needed to put first things first. What began to bother me though was seeing my peers complete this program. I became jealous as I went to their celebrations for obtaining the highest degree in the land. Jamie Wilson, Jayan Allen, Shelton Wright, Farrell Young, Wendolyn

Bouie, and Selina Thedford are a few of my peers that finished before me. However, this was a good type of jealousy. It motivated me to continue. I recall a conversation with one of my mentors, Dr. Bobby Jordan. He told me that when he was working on his doctorate, he had to sacrifice something.

After a year off, I was ready to make sacrifices to get this done. As a principal, my days and nights were full of activities. I thought long and hard on when and how I could put in some work. Since 1991, I have been working out at 5:30 AM with my best friends, Tony Owens, Al Ringer, and Major (Bull) Ealey. This was a time for us to bond and remain physically fit at the same time. As much as this meant to me, I decided to give it up. Instead of going to Lee Haney's World Class Fitness Center at 5:30 AM, I went to my office and Stone Mountain High School for two months. There, I would read, write, type, and do research on my topic.

On February 17, 2004, I entered the room as Mr. Simpson. The next hour will prove to be either completion of a monumental task or going back to the drawing board. I exited that same room as Dr. Ralph L. Simpson. I had earned a Doctorate in Educational Leadership from the University of Sarasota. My options went from two to two thousand. Neither of my parents had more than a high school diploma. Although both my brother and I were told that we needed to go to college, we lacked the necessary guidance to help prepare us for the next level. By the grace of God, I became the first and my family to obtain the doctorate degree. My 480 on the SAT was supposed to serve as an indicator as to whether I would graduate from college. However, the SAT does not measure DETERMINATION, DEDICATION, AND PERSEVERANCE. If that were the case, I would have had a perfect score of 1600. How can someone go from taking remedial courses in high school and college to earning the highest degree in the land? It is important for me to add that this degree does not define who I am. It only defines what I was able to achieve.

First and foremost, I have done nothing that any ordinary person cannot do. I am just an ordinary person who attempted to do extraordinary things. I was able to accomplish a lot with all of my challenges. Anything is possible! I am a real life example of an average student who chose not to quit. It is important to know that it does not matter where you start; what matters is where you finish. That's what happens when you GET IN THE WAY. Get in the way of an education, and before it is over, you will have achieved something to show for it. I challenge you to do what I did. Now how I did it, but better.

I once shared with one of my senior classes that I made a 480 on the SAT. They laughed so loud and long that it created a minor school disturbance. After order was restored, I challenged them to do what I did. I challenge them to skip or complete the 13th grade. Graduate from college with little or no preparation. Continue your pursuit in obtaining an advanced degree while facing the challenges of not being successful on standardized tests. Take those tests repeatedly after failing to meet the criteria. Face rejection from being accepted for admissions to a graduate program on two occasions. And finally, get in the way for four more years and obtain a doctorate degree. My closing statement to that senior class, "After you have done that, then you can laugh."

"My mother never gave up on me. I messed up in school so much they were sending me home, but my mother sent me right back."

Denzel Washington

Chapter Eleven

Braggin' Rights

All that I do is, truthfully, to give my mama some braggin' rights. For those that don't know, your parents brag about you and what you are doing. This is what they talk about on their jobs with co-workers as well with family members. I have yet to meet a parent who is not proud to share with others the good things that their children are doing. For the record, Roxie Mae Simpson is not the braggin' type. She has eleven brothers and sisters. If anyone decides that they want to share information about their children, I have given my mama enough good stuff to talk about. Every day, I continue to work hard so that I can impress her. I love making her feel proud.

Although my dad and I did not have the greatest relationship growing up, I knew that he loved me. It could be said that this was somewhat typical of that era. In my opinion, he was the best at providing for his family. My brother and I had everything we needed and most of what we wanted. For that, I have all the love and respect in the world for him. Much of my success can be attributed to his work ethic. That had a tremendous impact on me. I often heard of how Henry Simpson Jr. bragged on my brother and me. It is important that you give your parents something to brag about. Before making decisions that will result in an arrest, incarceration, or embarrassment, I think of how it is going to affect my family. You must first consider the consequences of your inappropriate actions.

This is the way conversations go with a group of your parents' friends or co-workers about their children. "My baby made the Honor Roll at her school!" "My son won first place in the Social Studies fair." If your parents have nothing to add to the conversation, all they can do is listen. They can't say anything about you because you have not given them anything to brag about. Remember, you have to give them a reason to brag about you. Begin today by working for things that your parents would be so proud to share with others that makes other people sick from hearing it so much.

More than anything, you owe it to your parents to become somebody. Think of all that they have done for you as a provider. How could you not repay them for all the sacrifices they made to make sure that you had everything you needed and most of the things you wanted? This is really not about you at all. They will not ask you for money like you asked them. They will not ask you to buy them material things. However, when Mother's Day and Father's Day roll around, ask them, "What is it that I can do for you?" After that, sit back and listen to them brag.

"Lots of people want to ride with you in the limo, but what you want is someone who will take the bus with you when the limo breaks down."

Oprah Winfrey

Conclusion

I take no credit for what I have done nor do I think that I am remarkable. However, what is remarkable is what I have been able to achieve. I give full credit to God who has given me the ability to do what I do. Just remember, if you are doing something positive, people will always talk about you. Don't worry about the haters. If they spend time talking about you or hating on you, obviously they like what you are doing. The Lord is remarkable in how he has blessed me with the gift to be able to remain a student-centered principal, a person who can speak the language of our youth while at the same time commanding the level of respect to guide, lead, and teach them to strive for excellence. This I know is a blessing from God. For me to experience this level of success in such a short period of time, I believe I was called to do what I do.

I feel ordained to share my experiences with children to encourage and motivate those that need a little push. It is my wish that I am able to continue in spreading my message from city to city, state to state, and school to school. I challenge everyone to find his or her niche. Find out what your purpose is in life. Everyone is good at something. Once you have done so, you will not hate school. You need to be prepared so that you can skip the 13th grade. Making good decisions will keep you out of the Lock Up. After you have done that, Get in the Way of an Education. Stand for Something! If you don't, you will fall for anything. Equip your parents with some Braggin' Rights. Regardless of what it is.

If you can't be a pine at the top of the hill,
    Be a shrub in the valley - but be
The best little shrub by the side of the rill;
    Be a bush if you can't be a tree.
If you can't be a bush, be a bit of the grass,
    And some highway happier make;
If you can't be a muskie, then just be a bass -
    But be the liveliest bass in the lake!
We can't all be captain; we've got to be crew,
    There's something for all of us here,
There's big work to do, and lesser to do,
    And the task you must do is the near.
If you can't be a highway, then just be a trail,
    If you can't be the sun, be a star;
It isn't by size that you win or you fail -
    Be the best of whatever you are!

By Douglas Malloch

www.ingramcontent.com/pod-product-compliance
Lightning Source LLC
Chambersburg PA
CBHW031426290426
44110CB00011B/548